Sister to Sister

Black Women
Speak to
Young Black Women

Beth Johnson

SISTER TO SISTER
Black Women Speak to Young Black Women

TP THE TOWNSEND LIBRARY

For more titles in the Townsend Library,
visit our website: www.townsendpress.com

Photo credits:
Marcia Lyles photo courtesy of Marcia Lyles
Julia Burney-Witherspoon photo by Mark Hertzberg
All other photographs by Beth Johnson

Lyrics to "No Mirrors in my Nana's House" are reprinted by permission
of the author. Words and music by Ysaye M. Barnwell, ©1992 Barnwell's
Notes Publishing, BMI/Harry Fox Agency

Townsend Press, Inc.
439 Kelley Drive
West Berlin, New Jersey 08091
cs@townsendpress.com

ISBN-13: 978-1-59194-204-7
ISBN-10: 1-59194-204-7

Library of Congress Control Number:
2009936317

CONTENTS

Introduction

Every girl sometimes needs a big sister to talk with. Big sisters can be a wonderful resource. They've been around the block a few times. They're willing to admit their own mistakes, to listen, to laugh and cry together, to give guidance, to talk about the (sometimes hard) lessons they've learned in life. They're a little like a mom and a little like a friend, but somehow they fill a role that is all their own. Most important, they know and love their younger sisters in a way no one else can.

The very special relationship that exists between older and younger sisters is the reason we've created the book you are holding in your hands. For *Sister to Sister: Black Women Speak to Young Black Women*, we invited ten remarkable women to open their hearts to the young "sisters" they imagine might be reading their words. Each woman was asked to speak freely on whatever topic she thought might be of interest and value to an African American girl growing up in America today.

Some of the contributors reflected on the whole of their life's journey. Others focused on a specific incident or period in their lives. Still others addressed a particular topic or idea. The essays are as diverse as the women who contributed them. In *Sister to Sister*, you will hear the voices of high school dropouts and the voices of women with doctor's degrees. There are women who became mothers at a very young age and mature women who have not yet chosen to have children. There are women who have lived in poverty and women who have grown up middle-class. There are women who have lived in the criminal underworld and women who have been community leaders. There are women who are known across the nation and women who are known only in their own communities. But all these women, no matter how different their life's journeys, have arrived at a place where they can look back and offer deep, thoughtful reflection upon what they have learned.

Why does *Sister to Sister* focus on the experiences of Black women? Certainly, women of all colors and cultures learn and benefit from the love and guidance of their older "sisters." But in looking at the media messages that bombard each of us every waking moment of our day, it seems clear that young Black girls are especially targeted by potentially destructive, soul-sucking images of what it means to be a Black women. Rather than providing a realistic view of Black women as being complex and multifaceted like everyone else, the media all too often present only a few "flavors" of African American females. We're all familiar with depictions of the gold-digging bitch, the crack whore, the welfare queen, the superhuman matriarch, and the booty-shaking rap-video dancer. A vulnerable young Black girl growing up on a steady diet of those images can too easily believe that those images represent the only choices available to her.

We hope that *Sister to Sister* will offer young Black readers an antidote to the poison of those lying—and limiting—images. You are warmly invited to spend time with ten remarkable women who have offered their sisterhood to you. As you read the words of Jean Sutton, Rasheedah Phillips, Yolanda Easley, Stephanie Wroten, Marcia Lyles, Julia Burney-Witherspoon, Kimberly Roberts, Mary Griffin, Hamidah Sharif-Harris, and Lina Buffington, you will be enriched by the broad spectrum of experience and diversity represented by today's Black women. Sit back, relax, and enjoy your time with these, your loving and caring big sisters.

Jean Sutton

About Jean Sutton

Jean Sutton was raised by her widowed mother in West Oak Lane, a mostly African American community in northwest Philadelphia. She attended Franklin & Marshall College, a primarily white college in rural Lancaster, Pennsylvania. It was at Franklin & Marshall that she met Rod Sutton, the man she would later marry. Rod's own story is told in *Brother to Brother: Black Men Speak to Young Black Men*, another book in the Townsend Library. Today Jean is an assistant vice president with Unitrin Direct, an insurance company, and Rod is an assistant principal at Philadelphia's University City High School. Jean and Rod are the parents of three children. In her essay, Jean writes about preparing for adult life, choosing a mate, and building a strong marriage.

Jean Sutton Speaks

"If I died, you'd have nothing. I have nothing to leave you."

Those are harsh words to hear when you're only 11, but I knew my mother was only telling me the truth.

"Don't make the same mistake I did," she said. "Educate yourself. Don't grow up expecting that a man will always provide for you. Anything can happen."

She knew what she was talking about. She had learned that lesson the hard way. With only an eighth-grade education, she had few job opportunities available to her. She provided childcare out of our home, a row house in a working-class neighborhood of Philadelphia. My father was a high school graduate who had joined the military, and had then gone to work in a steel plant.

Then my father died suddenly. My mother and I were forced onto the emotional roller coaster that follows the death of a loved one. Our sorrow was compounded by the financial impact of my father's loss. My mother struggled to make ends meet. We had to give up our car, and we very nearly lost our house. At a very early age, I realized how vulnerable an uneducated woman is.

I think that was my first lesson in selecting a mate and in preparing myself for adulthood. I learned that I wanted to be a financial equal in a marriage. I didn't want to have to marry in order to survive. I didn't want to be unable to support myself if my man was no longer around. I set about the task of becoming self-sufficient. I completed my formal education and am now an assistant vice president at an insurance company. I am happily married, but I have also prepared myself for life's unexpected events.

From my elementary years on, I was a good student. I enjoyed school, but beyond that, I never forgot that education would provide me with the opportunities my mother hadn't had. When it was time for college, Franklin & Marshall College in Lancaster, Pennsylvania, offered me a scholarship. F&M is a very good school with a small minority enrollment. When I attended, there were 1,500 students, of whom about 50 were African American. I had gone to a Catholic high school with white students, so being with white people was not that big a deal. For me, the adjustment was more about class than about race. In high school, we'd all worn uniforms, so it wasn't so obvious who had money and who didn't.

But at F&M I really saw the disparity. Now that I was living around people who had always had money, I felt poor in a way I never had before. My classmates were surprised that I took my work-study job in the cafeteria so seriously. If they had jobs, it was just to earn pocket money. But I needed my job so that I could buy a winter coat. In the summers I worked full-time in order to buy textbooks for the next year. Although I tried hard to find affordable used books, one year I ran out of money before the second semester began. That term I developed a new schedule. I would sleep in the evening while my dorm mates studied. Then I would borrow the books I needed and study through the night. I took special satisfaction in making the dean's list that term!

Sister to Sister

Because F&M didn't have a large enrollment of Black students, the Black Student Union made special efforts to help us get to know each other. The BSU assigned each of us incoming students a mentor, and early in my freshman year they hosted a dance. My mentor noticed me sitting on the sidelines and asked one of the older students to invite me to dance. That student was Rod Sutton, the man I would later marry. I told Rod that I didn't feel like dancing. He said, "Okay, but then I'm going to sit and talk with you."

What I first noticed about Rod was the same thing most people notice—that he's *big*: a big, tall man with a big voice. And being from inner-city Newark, New Jersey, he's very street savvy. As we sat and talked, however, I sensed that this big, loud guy was also kind and gentle. I felt a bond with him, as we had both grown up in the city without much money.

For a full year after that first meeting, Rod and I were just friends. Yes, for real, *friends*. And since I was just his friend, he wasn't trying to impress me. He was just being himself. During that year, we had long talks about how we wanted our lives to turn out. He talked about his plan to teach and to attend graduate school. He told me that he wanted to complete his education before he got married. He talked about the girls he'd known in his old neighborhood who had become teenage mothers, and how sad he was that those smart, talented girls would be unlikely to ever realize their full potential. He said he didn't want to bring a child into this world before he was ready to be a devoted, responsible parent.

Wow, I thought. Even as he was criticizing teenage pregnancy, he did it in a way that didn't trash the girls involved. He acknowledged that they were smart and talented. He respected them. That impressed me.

Other things impressed me as well. During our friendship, I had the chance to hang out with Rod and his friends. Many of those friends were good-looking guys, attractive and smart. But some were disrespectful of their own girlfriends or were involved in relationships built on guilt or control. Once I heard one of these guys call his girlfriend the "b" word right to her face. She shrugged it off as if it were nothing. Can you believe that the next day she was walking across the quad with him, arm in arm? When Rod heard such things, he always spoke up to the guy. He would criticize the disrespectful attitude toward "the young lady," as he always carefully referred to the girl.

As Rod and I exchanged our life stories, I came to respect him even more. I learned that this gentle, kind man had been an angry, troubled kid who had been repeatedly kicked out of school for fighting. He'd finally been sent to a kind of last-chance school, one run by monks. There, gradually, he had turned around. As I heard him talk about how his attitude had changed and as I watched him in his daily life, I could see he was for real. He was consistent in his actions as well as his words. He wasn't saying things because he thought they were what I wanted to hear. He didn't just talk the talk—he walked the walk.

We began to date, and my good opinion of Rod kept growing. After we graduated from F&M, he got a job teaching elementary school. He lived in Philly but commuted to Camden, New Jersey, every day. That first winter, the temperature fell to zero after a storm that dropped seven inches of snow. The schools in Philly and Camden were closed, but Rod left for work so early in the morning that he missed the announcement and drove all the way to Camden anyway. Here was a single guy, no wife or children to support, and yet he had such a strong work ethic he always showed up at work, often earlier than anyone else.

Watching him, I thought, He's hard-working, considerate, respectful, and a communicator. What more could a girl ask for?

Then I saw him interact with an elderly woman. When we were in a department store, Rod noticed her carrying a heavy shopping bag and struggling to open the door. "Let me help you with that, ma'am," he said. He took her bag and opened the door for her. "Thank you!" she said with a smile. He stood and watched her go until he was sure she was okay.

That sealed the deal for me. On top of everything else, he cared about our elderly! To this day, he dotes on the senior women in our church. He visits the sick and shut-ins. He goes beyond simply opening the door or helping with a bag. He engages them in a way that makes each one feel like the most important person in the world. I tease him about how he flatters the seniors, but I admire the care and respect that he shows. Given all the wonderful things I'd observed in Rod over the years, there was no question in my mind about what to say when he asked me to marry him.

My appreciation for his good qualities has only continued to grow since our wedding many years ago. Before my mother passed away, she was seriously ill for many months, and I was her sole caregiver. When I came down with the flu, Rod stepped in without hesitation. He visited her every single day, making sure she had a good meal and fresh water by her bedside. Some days he sat with her for hours, just to keep her company.

In parenthood, as well as elsewhere in our lives, Rod and I are true partners. We agreed that we wanted to wait to start our family until we felt really ready. I know that during the years before we had a child, Rod took some static from men he knew. They'd pressure him, saying things like "Don't you know how to make a baby?" They'd say it in a joking way, but you know a lot of guys would have been bothered by that. They were implying he wasn't a "real man" until he had fathered a child. But Rod never let such things get to him. He made it clear that *we* were going to make that decision; that we were a team, and that no outside pressure was going to influence us. I am so grateful that Rod felt the same way I did—that bringing a new human being into the world is a very serious decision, and not something to be done lightly.

We did make that decision in our own time, and our family now includes Paige, who is 13; Justin, 11; and Abu, an 8-year-old we're in the process of adopting. Abu has gone through a lot in his short life, and we are all excited about his move from the foster-care system to his forever home. In Rod's career as a teacher and now as an assistant principal, he has seen so many angry, scared, neglected children. He's worked very hard to help them, but as a teacher you can do only so much. We feel we've been very blessed in our own lives, and we've always wanted to share our good fortune with another child.

So by now you know that I'm a big fan of my husband and an advocate of marriage. But rest assured that marriage is not easy. It takes a lot of negotiating and hard work. That's why it is so important to have patience in selecting and getting to know your mate. You cannot get to know someone in a day, a week, or even a month. It takes time. A good rule of thumb is to know your mate through at least four seasons before you get married. Don't rush!

And don't just listen to what a guy *says*. Words are easy. Observe his *actions*. Observe how he treats his family and close friends. That will be a good indication of how he'll treat you.

I see so many of the girls I grew up with settle for, in my opinion, far less than they deserve. We African American women face some special challenges. To begin with, we simply outnumber our marriageable men. So many of our men are in prison. And there is a widespread perception that high-achieving Black men don't marry Black women, that they go outside the race. I don't know how true that is, but many women believe it.

So I think a lot of women end up saying, "Well, this guy is halfway decent and not in prison," and they settle. And the result is so much divorce and so many children growing up without fathers. I understand why it happens. When your friends are getting married and having babies, it's easy to get swept up in the excitement of that. You don't want to be left behind. But marriage and parenthood are too important to go into for less than the right reasons.

I am convinced that good men, loving men, dependable men who hold themselves to high standards, are out there. Hold out! Give it time. Look in the right places—places like school, church, and work. I'll tell you where *not* to look—in bars and clubs. Sure, a good guy could be at a club. But in general, guys hanging out in clubs are looking for someone for a while, not for a lifetime.

Ladies, love yourself enough to, first, be the best person that you can be. Then love yourself enough to demand of your partner all that is rightfully yours. Take the time to be certain that the love you have is a love that will always be there. I'm not talking about the sexy love of your youth. I'm talking about a love that will be there at the end of your life, holding your hand when you take your last breath—a love that endures not only through joy and fun, but also through sickness and despair and whatever life may bring. Do not settle for less. Love yourself enough to hold out for all that you deserve.

Rasheedah Phillips

About Rasheedah Phillips

Rasheedah was the daughter of a fourteen-year-old mother. Her childhood was unstable. There wasn't any money. She and her mother lived with a variety of relatives. She attended three elementary schools and two middle schools. So when Rasheedah herself became pregnant at 14, the world was ready to write her off as another sad inner-city statistic. However, Rasheedah refused to be written off. Taking on an attitude of "no excuses for failure," she finished high school. She completed her college degree in three years, instead of the usual four. She earned a law degree from Temple University. Today this former teen mom is a lawyer helping families in need through Philadelphia's Community Legal Services. She and her daughter Iyonna, now 10, share a home in Philadelphia.

Rasheedah Phillips Speaks

Little Lady, you come in all different colors, shapes, and sizes. But no matter what you look like, you must still deal with the growing pains of becoming a young woman. You watch TV and see "role models" who wear halter tops and booty shorts, inject plastic into their breasts, and worship the video "hos," the Lil' Kims and Karrine

"Superhead" Steffans of the world. Little Lady, when you get on the bus to go to school, you are surrounded by street-corner crack houses disguised as fast food restaurants, "restaurants" whose "food" pollutes your body with hormones, assigning curves to your hips before they are due. Your world can seem confusing at best, and often bleak and without promise.

But, Little Lady, did you know that you live in a world where possibilities are vast, endless, and infinite? It doesn't seem that way, does it? Especially when your skin is not the "right" color, or your hair isn't the "right" texture, or you aren't the "right" weight, or because you are a girl and not a guy, or because you are a girl who likes girls instead of guys. It's easy to focus in negative ways on the traits that set you apart from the crowd. Sometimes it seems as if those differences create barriers in your life, but you must be strong and knock those barriers down! Stand tall, and be proud of your differences. They are the things that make you beautiful and memorable. How boring would the world be if we all looked and acted the same? How dull would the world be if it didn't have you? Embrace and hold tight to what makes you unique. Don't let what the world thinks dictate your future!

You see, Little Lady, I am not too far removed from you. Though I am where I am now—a college graduate and a lawyer—it was only a few years ago that I stood in your shoes, sat in your seat. I know where you come from. I was there with you.

Many of us were forced to mature at a very young age. I know I was. Many of us have faced responsibilities and situations that we shouldn't have had to face. Many of us had to give up our childhood before we even had a chance to taste it. Many of us made wrong choices and mistakes—sometimes because of the limited number of choices that we had, and sometimes because we could not recognize the opportunities that *did* exist. Many of us are part of a vicious, oppressive cycle—a cycle of poverty, drugs, teen parenthood, abuse, absent parents, gangs, jail, and unemployment. We come from desolate neighborhoods filled with hopelessness, frustration, desperation. We are the products and victims of inequality, racism, classism, sexism, and elitism. We come from schools with outdated books, crowded classrooms, limited resources, and low expectations. We are told in both spoken and silent ways that we will never measure up to our suburban counterparts. Having been assigned the label "inner-city," we are invisible, unnoticed. We have been stripped of our identities and handed a warped self-image, unequal education, and few opportunities. We have been told that we won't amount to much, that we can't get very far, and that we have no worth or value. Most tragically, we have internalized these views, adopted them as our own.

Is it possible to reject those views, to create a different reality? It is, Little Lady. I promise you that it is. I had my daughter Iyonna, who is now 10, when I was fourteen years old. As a young single mother, I was forced to mature very early, facing responsibilities that many adolescents do not have to face. Coming from a long line of teen mothers, I realized that my daughter's fate was in my hands. If I was going to break the family cycle, I had to give Iyonna a more stable life than my mother had been able to provide for me. It was my job to give her as many options as possible for her future and her education.

In the beginning, I felt discouraged by the countless negative stereotypes about teen parents—that we cannot amount to much and that we have no value to society. I chose not to internalize those views, not to allow my status as a teenage mother to define or confine me. Instead, I used it as motivation to overachieve and rise above the expectations that others had of me. My experiences with juggling school, work, and a child during high school fully prepared me for the numerous responsibilities I would later face in college and law school.

Even with my mom to help me, caring for a baby while I was in high school was not an easy feat. I began every day at 6:00 a.m. to prepare myself for school and Iyonna for daycare. Boarding the bus with a stroller, a diaper bag on my shoulder, and a book bag on my back, I dropped Iyonna off and got back on the bus to go to school all day. After school, I had to pick Iyonna back up to take her home, then go to work for four hours a night. Getting back home at 9:00 p.m., I was met at the door with a baby and homework, which often kept me up until 1:00 or 2:00 in the morning and resulted in my getting an average of four hours of sleep per night.

In spite of my hectic schedule, I was able to attain my degrees with my daughter in tow. Along the way, the example that I set was instilling in *her* a strong sense of confidence. I was able to prove that having a child at a young age does not have to mean a dead end to your own achievement. As challenging as young motherhood is, it can motivate and inspire a young woman to succeed.

Little Lady, you may not be a teenage parent, and your struggles may not look like mine, but I know you have your own obstacles before you. In order to overcome them, you must set your goals, and then see those goals as achievable. You must believe that they are within your reach if you stretch your arms to grasp them. If you maintain your focus, nothing can deter you from achieving your dreams. Out of the abyss of negative labels—the sea of harmful circumstances that threaten to pull you under—you will emerge triumphant. You—yes, *you*—can rise up to contradict what others believe is the destiny of so-called poor, inner-city women of color. You can prove that you do not have to give in to your environment and that you do not have to let challenges beat you down and run you over.

There are three things that I want to emphasize to you, Little Lady, as you are mapping out your future course in life: *abilities, dreams,* and *responsibilities.* Stevie Wonder once said, "We all have ability. The difference is how we use it." All of us have some sort of talent or ability that we can utilize to help ourselves and to help others. You may be talented at painting, writing, singing, or even listening to others and giving advice. You can use these talents to advance your career or to communicate and teach others—and to make your unique mark on the world.

As a child, I knew that I wanted to be a writer and that I wanted to create stories. But I never had anyone tell me that I could be an author when I grew up, that this was a realistic dream for a little Black girl living in a bad neighborhood. However, as I grew older, there were a few special people in my life who recognized my abilities and who encouraged me to nurture those abilities and use them to achieve my goals. My ability to write and to put my ideas down on paper gave me the chance to earn scholarships and recognition in contests. I even had the opportunity to be published in an anthology of short stories and poems called *Growing Up Girl.* Today I continue to nurture my love of writing by taking creative writing classes in my spare time. Also, as an attorney, I must be a strong writer in order to advocate for my clients and get them the things they need.

Your next step is to set goals for putting your ability to use, or to enhance your ability by continuing your education. Only by forming and fulfilling those goals will you ever be able to achieve your dreams. Dreams are essential to a productive life. As poet Langston Hughes said:

> *Hold fast to dreams*
> *For if dreams die*
> *Life is a broken-winged bird*
> *That cannot fly*

However, once you begin to turn those dreams into reality, you must never say, "There; now I'm finished." Constantly remind yourself of what you can still achieve. The moment that you become complacent is the moment that your dreams die, that you stop trying, that you awaken in your bed to find that the world has passed you by. Never stop striving, never accept what is given to you without question. Go for it all. The only things that stand in your way are the limitations that you impose on yourself. I think the comedian and actor Dwayne Kennedy was right when he said, "Internal barriers are much more difficult to overcome than the external ones." We may not have physical shackles any longer, but we are still too often oppressed by mental shackles.

Those mental shackles are restraints that were being forged before we were born. As so-called minorities and poor people, we are part of a despised socioeconomic underclass. There are no white picket fences in our neighborhoods, no two-parent families with 2.5 children. In many cases, we are raised in conditions that are the opposite of the American Dream. Yet we are told we should achieve that dream, even though we lack the means to do so. We are pushed to achieve that dream while being told that we are less worthy of it than others in better circumstances. Our American dream has become an American nightmare. We have been endowed with what W.E.B. Du Bois called a "double consciousness," and those two aspects of consciousness are in a constant tug of war. One tells us that we must achieve that dream, while the other pushes us to remain true to our own culture.

It is your task to reconcile and resolve that double consciousness so that your understandable frustration does not stand in the way of your achievement. As Malcolm X once said, you must "Be very careful about letting others make up your mind for you." You must reconcile those mixed messages you have received all your life and move toward your goal with steady determination.

It will not always be easy. Despite your best efforts, the road will not be smooth. There will be potholes along the way—and detours. You will continue to face challenges and obstacles. You will continue to make mistakes. But our mistakes can shape us and become our learning experiences. I like to remember what John Powell, an English composer, wrote: "The only real mistake is the one from which we learn nothing."

Once you are on your way to turning your dreams into reality, it is then time for you to face your responsibilities—to yourself, to your family, to your community, to those who have paved the way for you, and to those for whom you will pave the way. It is our job to become role models for the next generation. Our ancestors and our teachers have played their part. It is our turn to stand up and shape the future.

Sister to Sister

Finally, Little Lady, when it all seems like it is too much for you to bear, please let me offer you strength and encouragement. In the dark moments, I hope you will look to the light that lies ahead. When I was in high school, as I looked back at hard times and realized that I was stronger than they were, I wrote the following passage. I invite you to take these words as your own:

I am a creature with a soul that may be bruised and scarred, with a heart that may be burned and scorned, with a nature that may be tested and scrutinized, but I will always emerge as triumphant. Others may deny me and I may deny myself, but at the end of the day, I am human, and that always means that tomorrow is a new day, another chance to start over and try my best to succeed.

Yolanda Easley

About Yolanda Easley

Yolanda Easley didn't set out to be a Black activist. But when she found herself one of only a few Black students at her college, she realized she had a job to do. She could help educate the students around her about her race and culture. In doing so, she found a part of herself that she hadn't known was missing. Today Yolanda is a teacher at a Philadelphia elementary school that serves mostly Hispanic families. Once again, she is in a position to participate in a cultural give-and-take that benefits everyone involved.

Yolanda Easley Speaks

I did not find myself until I began college. I thought I'd always known who I was and what I stood for, but those affirmations were never put to the test until I was placed in an unfamiliar environment.

I grew up in North Philadelphia, where I attended Gideon Elementary School and Strawberry Mansion Middle High School. During those years, the only people of different races I dealt with were my teachers and doctors. I say this to explain that while I have always known I was Black, my race wasn't something that I needed to think about very much. Being of a particular race took a back seat to my personality, demeanor, character, and upbringing.

My four years at Gettysburg College made me far more aware of my race than I had ever been before. When I visited the school, located more than 100 miles west of Philadelphia, the students of color were so welcoming and united that I didn't realize how few of them there were. My first night as a freshman was an eye-opening experience. After my family left, I went to the dining hall to get something to eat. For probably the first time in my life, I was the only Black person in the room. I remember looking around for someone who looked like me—and seeing no one. I felt so out of place and alone.

The first couple of months were hard, very hard. I kept to myself; I constantly called my family at home. More than once I felt that I wanted to leave. Luckily, I had a supportive family who reminded me how hard I had worked to get to Gettysburg and who reassured me that I could succeed there. My Grandma Sue especially encouraged me to hang in there. When I had been planning to go to college, I had considered Temple University, a large, diverse school right there in Philadelphia. But Grandma had advised me to go to Gettysburg. She said, "Get the experience. You'll grow by being away from home."

Yolanda Easley

In the long run, Grandma was absolutely right. But the adjustment wasn't easy. I had to slowly become comfortable with being the only Black person in my classes, the last person picked during group projects, the first name my professors remembered, and the loner frequently wandering around campus. I gradually began to open up to other people instead of walking around with my cell phone—my lifeline to home—clamped to my ear. And generally, it was fine. People weren't hostile, even the people who didn't pick me for group projects. They were just staying in their comfort zones.

But what drove me crazy was suddenly being "the Black girl." I felt as though I was wearing a sign with those words on it. It made me indignant that it wasn't enough to see me as smart, or honest, or kind, or hardworking. Sometimes it happened in ways that I couldn't believe. Early in my freshman year I was sitting in a class when the professor said, "Let's ask Yolanda to give us the Black perspective on this issue." I was absolutely floored. What was he *thinking*? So many possible responses went through my mind. Should I just throw out some answer and get the glare of the spotlight off me? Or should I speak my mind and feed into some stereotype of the "angry Black woman"? I compromised—I gave an answer but added that I could speak only for myself. I assumed that this was just a weird incident that would never happen again, but I was wrong. I remember at least three more times being asked in class for "the Black point of view." Uh, yeah—one nineteen-year-old woman can speak for an entire race of people, right? It was tough enough to be the black dot on the white page, as my friends and I would sometimes joke, but to be expected to speak on behalf of all African Americans was ridiculous.

By my second year of college, however, I quit fighting the inevitable battle of being Black on a predominately white campus, and chose to embrace the opportunity that the situation provided. I realized that much of my early isolation came from my own fear of not being accepted by the larger group. I was constantly worried that I couldn't just be me. Gradually that fear passed as I accepted the idea that, yes, in the context of Gettysburg College I *was* "the Black girl," and that was okay. Yes, my skin is dark. Yes, my hair is a different texture. Yes, I say "gonna" instead of "going to" and "ain't" instead of "isn't" and "axed" instead of "asked." And that's all okay, too! When you're only with people like you, you don't realize that how you look, act, speak, and relate are all part of your culture, and that you can take responsibility for educating others about that culture instead of trying to deny that those things matter.

Yolanda Easley

In order to increase other students' awareness of Black culture, a couple of friends and I formed the Diaspora House. This was a theme house for a group of students who promoted diversity and cultural awareness around the campus. We partnered with the college board in promoting a five-year plan to increase diversity on campus by working closely with the college admissions office and by volunteering to host overnight stays for prospective students of color. We posted "Did You Know" signs around the campus, inviting our white counterparts to educate themselves on a little African American history. We also held discussions on Black topics such as hair, color, and body image. Again, having come out of a community that was totally Black, I was amazed at some of the misunderstandings that came up. For instance, over Easter break one year I got micro braid hair extensions. When I got back to campus, some white girls said, "Oh my God, your hair grew so much!" I said, "Do you *really* think my hair could have grown five inches in four days?" But I think they really weren't sure—maybe they thought Black hair could do that! It was only at these meetings at the Diaspora House that the students of color outnumbered the white students. I refused to just quietly accept ignorance, so as a group, we pressed on. We came to the conclusion that if we were not heard by the audience we desired, we should continue with the audience that we had!

My greatest challenge in college was not a personal attack on me, but an attack on my race and culture. It was a clash that the students of color dreaded and hoped would never happen. One of my friends was verbally assaulted on campus by a white student who called her the "n" word. I had grown up in a community where the "n" word was used frequently by Black people toward other Blacks as a sign of respect and friendship. I had never before personally experienced it being used as a weapon of hatred and degradation.

As a group, the students of color were outraged. Because there were so few of us, we were already at the brink of revolt, and this incident brought us to the point of rioting. We sought help from the few Black administrators on our campus. They met with us at the Diaspora House and allowed us to vent our feelings. For the first time since I began college, I felt able to express myself around my superiors without fear of misinterpretation or racial bias. This was the first time that I felt free to be me!

Today I am an elementary teacher in a school that serves mostly Hispanic children. Of my fellow teachers, three are African American and nineteen are Hispanic. Once again I am in the minority. But this time I am fully comfortable with that fact—because I'm comfortable with who I am.

As ironic as it may sound, Gettysburg College introduced me to my Blackness. My experiences there made me conscious of my race and culture. I was presented with obstacles that challenged who I was and what many of my ancestors had fought for. I realized that being of a certain race does define you to an extent, and it does count for just as much of your being as your character does. Being Black in a white institution is not something that I've ever been ashamed of. Being a minority is something that can isolate and divide, yet it is also something that has made me stronger, prouder, and more conscious of my race and culture. Thus, I am stronger, prouder and more conscious of who I really am!

Stephanie Wroten

About Stephanie Wroten

Stephanie Wroten grew up in a predominately African American community. But when it was time for high school, her parents sent her to a college prep school where almost all the other students were white. The experience gave Stephanie valuable insight into the challenges facing people of color who find themselves living and working in a mostly white environment. Stephanie, a registered nurse with a master of science degree, is coordinator for multicultural student development at the Abington Memorial Hospital Dixon School of Nursing in Willow Grove, Pennsylvania. She and her husband Charles, a police officer, have two sons, Charles Jr. and Elijah.

Stephanie Wroten Speaks

I am a registered nurse. I work as the outreach coordinator for multicultural student development at a nursing school. It's my job to encourage minority students to consider nursing as a profession. Once they enroll, I offer academic and personal support.

I find that a really big issue for African American students at the school is assimilation—feeling comfortable as part of the larger group. Many of the students are entering a mostly white environment for the first time. They are being forced far out of their comfort zone. It can be very scary. I understand that because I went through that process at an earlier age.

I grew up in the West Oak Lane area of Philadelphia. Our neighborhood was all African American. My sisters and I were fortunate enough to have a very warm, supportive home. Dad worked as an engineer at the University of Pennsylvania hospital. He hadn't gone beyond high school, but he could fix anything. He kept the machines at the hospital running. He had a tremendous work ethic. Mom had attended college for a while, and she worked as a teacher's assistant in the city.

I went to grade school at a local Catholic school whose students were mostly Black. When it came time for high school, most of my classmates went to the nearest Catholic high school. But my parents said, "We want more for you." They sent me, as they had my sisters before me, across town to Mount St. Joseph Academy, or "the Mount," an all-girls college prep school. To get to the Mount, we Black students had to catch a city bus and ride all the way to the end of the line. Then we would get off and walk through a patch of woods to get to the campus. We followed a path worn down by other city girls who had made that trek over the years. In our graduating class of 125 girls, nine were African American.

Stephanie Wroten

During my first month at the Mount, I thought my parents had definitely lost their minds. Instead of being with the kids I'd gone to school with all my life, I was with girls who were not only white but who came from some of the most affluent families in Philadelphia. These were girls who got Volvos or diamond rings for their sixteenth birthday. Many of them were "legacies," meaning their grandmothers or great-grandmothers had attended the school. So it was like living two lives. All day I'd be rubbing shoulders with these very affluent, bright, privileged white girls. Then I'd get back on that city bus and return to my working-class African American neighborhood.

For the most part, people were nice enough. The real day-to-day problem was that there was no validation of who I was. There were no Black teachers, no Black administrators. There was no one to say, "Stephanie, here is *your* history, *your* family, *your* culture." The school marked Martin Luther King's birthday, but that was the end of its acknowledgment of African Americanism. It was up to me to fit in with them.

And occasionally, hostility would break through. Strangely enough, the very worst incident occurred during my Senior Week, just after graduation. Many of us had gone down to the Jersey Shore to celebrate. A group of us Black girls walked into one party, and one of the white girls looked up and said, "Oh, look who's here. It's the niggers." I'd known her since freshman year. I'd been in her homeroom. I said, "Wow. You've waited *four years* to say that. I hope you're happy." Then I turned and left.

But overall, the experience at Mount St. Joseph was extremely valuable to me. I don't know how to say it better than this: It polished me. At the Mount, I learned to attend a dinner party. I went to the opera and learned to appreciate classical music. I was taught to balance a checkbook and prepare a resumé and organize my calendar. Ninety-nine percent of the girls who attended the Mount were going on to college. They were going to become professionals, have careers. It was understood that we needed this kind of preparation for life.

By learning those skills, I became a chameleon—you know, one of those lizards that can blend in with its surroundings. I gained the ability to move between my two worlds and to function well in both. Now, some Black people see learning those skills as selling out, as giving up who you are in order to try to be white. But that is not what it is at all. Why should education and success and culture be white things? I think the opposite is true. We weren't "acting white." In learning to negotiate that unfamiliar world, we became comfortable and secure in ourselves. Looking back, I can truthfully say that I would not change a moment of my experience. I am proud of the person I am today. The painful or difficult parts, as well as the good parts, made me who I am.

My father died when I was a junior in high school. Even as sick as he was, I always thought he was going to get better. He had genetic heart disease; he'd smoked all his life, he had diabetes, he ate all the wrong things. But in my eyes, he was invincible. It was the experience of seeing the doctor and nurses care for him in the hospital that made me want to become a nurse.

I enrolled at Germantown Hospital's school of nursing. It was there that I met Miss Mildred Howie, the first African American nurse educator I'd ever seen. I couldn't take my eyes off Miss Howie, I thought she was so great. And she made a great difference in my life. Here's what happened: We nursing students took our classes at La Salle University and our nursing instruction at Germantown. And at La Salle—well, I was nineteen years old and *very* social. The other nursing students would be in their rooms studying while I was getting to know everyone on campus. I knew the basketball team, the African American cultural clubs—I knew what was going *on*. I was having a great time. But I was just squeaking by academically.

One day, as I dashed into the dorm, I ran into Miss Howie. She could tell I'd been out having a good time.

And, of course, she'd seen my grades. Miss Howie took me by the hand and said, "Stephanie, you can't do this until you believe in yourself more than I do."

It wasn't a huge conversation. It was a brief interaction in the hallway. But it changed my life. I wasn't doing what I was supposed to do, and she called me on it. She made me realize it wasn't enough to *say* I wanted to be a nurse. I had to work for it.

There are different ways of making that point with people. Miss Howie did it her way. By contrast, there was my academic advisor. During my "social" period, I failed an important test. I had been out late the night before, and my scores showed it. My advisor took the test, threw it down on the desk between us, and said, "These scores make the difference between those who *run* a floor and those who *mop* the floor."

That hit me hard, because the fact was—and she knew it—that my Uncle Dove *did* mop floors right there at that hospital. And by mopping those floors, he raised five children and did a beautiful job of it. I was proud of Uncle Dove, and he was so proud to have me there as a student. And here was this white woman standing there and saying, in so many words, "You can't do it."

Yes, I had failed the test. Yes, that was my fault. But her response was so insulting. She could have said what needed to be said in a far less hurtful way. I stood up and said, "You cannot be my advisor anymore." I asked to be reassigned and, thank heavens, I got Miss Howie.

I often remember those two incidents in the job I have today. To be a successful mentor, you need to choose your words carefully. You can do so much damage in a careless moment. So I speak very clearly to students about consequence and personal responsibility. I make sure they understand that academic failure means they will not be here anymore and that they will be stuck in some less fulfilling job. But destroy a student's confidence? Shatter her self-esteem? No, I don't go there.

Because all students are fragile. And minority students are often especially fragile. My students don't always ask the questions that need to be asked, because they're afraid to reveal what they don't know. They're not sure they deserve to be here. It's part of my job to build their confidence, to convince them that they deserve to be here as much as anyone does.

But it's not easy. Our students are suffering. The school systems are failing them and, often, their families are failing them. They lack social skills, organizational skills, math skills, and reading comprehension skills. They've been passed along from grade to grade despite their lack of those fundamentals. They're shocked and upset when they find out that they're not prepared for the work they need to do. It's hard on me and hard on them when they look around and say, "How come everybody but me can do this?" So we meet them where they are. If we need to start with 1 + 1, that's what we do.

It can be just as frustrating when students *are* doing well and do not receive support. I tell my African American students again and again "No one is asking you to change who you are inside. You are *not* betraying yourself by learning to act professionally." Unfortunately they may go back to their neighborhoods, where they get flak and hear "Now you think you're white." That comparison is baloney. There's nothing "white" about speaking like you're educated and carrying yourself with confidence and self-esteem. But those are hurtful words to hear. I know it. I dealt with them myself. I see a big part of my job as helping my students become comfortable with success. I tell them, "You have to *own* that success. It doesn't come easy. You have to work hard to achieve it. And when you achieve it, you should be very proud. Don't let anyone tell you differently."

My sistahs, it takes extreme courage to maintain a standard. Please love who you are, identify your standards, and respect yourself. Love yourself more than men, more than material possessions, and more than society's perception of success. Understand that your mental and physical health are vital to achieving balance in your life. Always aim high or just do your best for the given moment. The small successes matter! Education provides you with options and endless power.

Not every experience is a life-or-death matter. Don't be rendered powerless by the negative aspects of your journey. Savor each pitfall as the path that will lead you to knowing inner peace. Love your life and take time to experience each moment. We are gifted. Instill in your children the importance of character, honor, education, prayer, and family. Life experiences will make you wise. Most of all, Sistahs, hold each other's hands, have each other's backs, and whisper "I love you" in one another's ears. I love you, my sistahs, mothers, aunts, nieces, cousins, friends, and teachers! I love each of you.

Marcia Lyles

About Marcia Lyles

When Marcia Lyles was appointed New York City Deputy Chancellor for Teaching and Learning in 2007, the school system was getting an administrator who knew it from the inside out. Born in Harlem, Dr. Lyles has lived in every one of the city's boroughs over the course of her sixty years. She began her career as a high school English teacher and was later a regional superintendent for New York City Public Schools, overseeing 150 schools in Brooklyn with 80,000 students. Her latest position is Superintendent of Christina School District in the state of Delaware. Her ability to tackle tough educational problems reflects the story she tells here—her own experience as a student who was very nearly lost in the system.

Marcia Lyles Speaks

I wanted to be a teacher ever since I was in second grade. At that time I wanted to be—guess what—a second-grade teacher. The next year I wanted to be a third-grade teacher. After that, a fourth-grade teacher. You get the idea. My first class was made up of my dolls. I'd line them up and teach them and give them tests. I was tough! Some of them passed, and some of them did *not*.

Sister to Sister

I was born in Harlem, but in the course of growing up I lived in every borough in New York City. That is because I lost my mother when I was very young, only 10, and after that I was passed around by my relatives, from house to house. My father was supportive and I saw him every week, but by himself he wasn't able to care for a young girl.

The frequent moving made me unhappy. Looking back, I think my relatives were really just trying to find the best fit for me, but it was hard being uprooted again and again. And, of course, I missed my mother. I had a brother, but he was nine years older, so I felt like an only child. We were very poor, but I didn't realize that. As the youngest child, and the only girl, I'm sure I was pampered quite a lot. But after my mother's death, as I moved between these different homes, I was not an only child, and not the baby. I felt lost; I had the middle-child blues. In the home where I spent the longest time, the younger boy was blind, so he received a good deal of attention. For me, that was actually good, because I was able to help him and learn some teaching skills from the situation. I took him to music lessons and learned to play chess using Braille pieces.

My relatives were supportive of education, although they weren't highly educated themselves. My mother had dropped out of school and had her first child when she was only 14 or 15, but she was an avid reader. To this day, I love reading mystery novels, as she did. She just ate up the Perry Mason stories.

I did well in school. In fact, I skipped a year. Without a doubt, the most important influence in my school life was Mrs. Carrie Simpson, my sixth-grade teacher. It was Mrs. Simpson who made me begin to understand the power of expectations—that if you *expect* great things of a young person, you're more likely to *get* great things. I was positive I was her favorite student. I've discovered in later years, as I've talked to my fellow students from that year, that *every one* of us believed we were her favorite. We'll argue about it to this day. One will say, "Mrs. Simpson liked me best." Another will say, "Ex*cuse* me, but she liked *me* best." That is the kind of teacher she was!

I came into Mrs. Simpson's class shortly after my mother died. The entrance examination was coming up for Hunter College High School, a school for gifted students. Mrs. Simpson was determined that at least one of her students was going to get in. To be allowed to take the Hunter entrance exam, you had to score above a certain level on the IQ test. I took the test, but missed the cut-off by a few points. Mrs. Simpson somehow convinced the school that my score was low because I was mourning my mother, and they let me take the test again. That next time I scored high enough to take the entrance exam. I didn't get into Hunter, but I never forgot that Mrs. Simpson thought I was worth going to that trouble. (One of my classmates *did* get in. She is now a dean of John Jay College of Criminal Justice.)

Mrs. Simpson did other very special things, too. Our school was in Spanish Harlem, and Mrs. Simpson thought that since we lived in that area, we really ought to learn Spanish. So over lunch, on her own time, she gave us Spanish lessons. When we all came back from taking the Hunter College entrance exam, she asked how we had done. Several of us mentioned having trouble with one of the readings that included the word "nocturnal," which we didn't understand. She said, "Don't you remember when I taught you to say *good night* in Spanish—*buenas noches?* Look how the words *noches* and *nocturnal* are similar. If you had thought of that, you could have guessed that *nocturnal* means 'happening at night.'"

That idea—that one word could help you figure out another word—excited me. Mrs. Simpson had that gift for inspiring students to learn.

Even though we were only in sixth grade, Mrs. Simpson insisted that we start thinking about applying to college. She told each of us to write letters to several colleges asking for admissions material. I did, and one of the schools that responded was Fredonia College, way up in northwestern New York State. Years later, I actually went to college at Fredonia. I arrived there in February when it was 4 degrees Fahrenheit with eighteen inches of snow on the ground. I shared a house with ten white women, one of whom immediately told me, "You need to know that I don't like Black people, so stay away from me." But that's another story.

What I'm saying is that in a perfect world every child would have a series of teachers like Mrs. Simpson. She believed in every child and demonstrated that belief in her expectations of us. She moved heaven and earth in order to give us a taste of success, which she knew could inspire us in life-changing ways.

I started high school at Benjamin Franklin High School in my Harlem neighborhood. Oh, I did well there. I did very well. I did so well that I could play hooky on a regular basis and *still* do well. I knew exactly when I could cut and what I could cut, and I took full advantage. We were allowed to leave the school for lunch, and I often didn't return. Still, I had no problem keeping up with my assignments and staying at the top of my class.

Then my aunt found out that I was skipping school. She pulled me out of Ben Franklin and enrolled me way across town, in Queens, at Jamaica High School. How did I feel about that? Absolutely miserable. I had no friends at Jamaica. I felt estranged from my community, as I didn't get home until late in the day. I wasn't part of the crowd anymore. And while Benjamin Franklin had been almost entirely Black and Hispanic, Jamaica was at least 90 percent white. In my college prep classes at Jamaica, I was usually the only African American.

And the work was *incredibly* hard. When I started at Jamaica, the shock was tremendous. In East Harlem, I was an honor student with a very high grade point average (GPA). I could just sail along on my natural intelligence, playing hooky and whatever. At Jamaica— oh my God. The courses had names similar to the ones I'd been taking at Ben Franklin, but the content was much, much more difficult. I realized that I was far behind the other students and that I was going to have to work extremely hard to catch up. Ultimately, I was able to, but the adjustment was very difficult. I actually failed my first world history test, and I was not used to failure.

In hindsight, as unhappy as it made me, going to Jamaica was the best thing that could have happened to me—for a number of reasons. Up to that point in my life, I had had very little exposure to white people. But now I was with whites almost exclusively. I had to learn to interact with people who did not look like me, whose experiences had been very different from mine. I was very uncomfortable at first, but over time things got better. And now I really am one of those people who says, "Some of my best friends are . . ."

But the really big difference was this: For the first time, I was in an environment where people did not expect much of me. To get right to the point, they didn't expect much of me because I was Black. I had to fight for recognition of my ability at Jamaica. When I wasn't assigned to the college prep classes, I had to go to the teachers and the department heads and say, "I'm supposed to be in those classes. What do I have to do to convince you?" I had to argue for my place. To learn to do that, at age 14, was a very powerful experience. I had to stand up to people who did not want me at the table, or at least thought that I did not have what it took to be there. And I had to do that fighting myself. My family knew the importance of education, but they didn't really know the details, the importance of placement in certain classes.

It wasn't like I was treated with open hostility. Generally, that didn't happen. But there were moments of tension. I remember one rich white girl commenting in a snide way on my "Southern accent." Excuse me? Not only was *I* born in New York, but my *mother* was born in New York. We didn't talk "Southern." We talked like Black people. And in a class called Problems of Democracy—this was during the Vietnam War, and there was a lot to talk about—some students acted surprised that I could discuss the issues knowledgeably. It was obvious that they did not expect a Black girl to read the newspapers, watch the news, know what was going on in the world.

The point is this: At my old school, filled with minority kids, expectations for the students *as a whole* were low. For me as an individual they were higher, but the bar was still set pretty low. At this college-prep white school, expectations for the students as a whole were very high. But for me, as a Black student from Harlem, they were low. This was my first exposure to the different expectations for white and minority students. And I realized that if I had remained at Benjamin Franklin High School, I would have drifted down the road of mediocrity. I would not have known any better. The same thing is still happening to far too many of our minority students. Even the brightest of them are being let down by their schools' low expectations. They may make high grades and think everything is fine until they enter college and realize how poorly prepared they are.

In my career, I have been a teacher, a principal, a superintendent, Deputy Chancellor for Teaching and Learning for the City of New York, and now superintendent of a school district in Delaware. But fundamentally, I am still and always a teacher. As teachers, we want to support kids, but we don't always want to do what Carrie Simpson did—that is, do the difficult work of holding them to high standards. The problem is that the *world* will hold them to high standards. If we do anything less, we are letting those kids down.

What can you do for yourself if you're a student in a school that has low expectations of you? Of course, if you can somehow get yourself transferred to a more challenging school, that's an option. But beyond that, you may need to take the lead in navigating your own path. Reach out to adults in your world who have an interest in encouraging and supporting you. Ask them to help you search out special opportunities, such as enrichment programs in your community. Don't settle for classes that are easy for you; challenge yourself with the ones that really make you work. Realize that the "mean teachers" may actually have the most to offer you. If people in your life have high expectations of you, that can make all the difference. Finally, the most important person to have high expectations of you is *you*.

Julia Burney-Witherspoon

About Julia Burney-Witherspoon

As the oldest of twelve children growing up in Racine, Wisconsin, Julia Burney-Witherspoon learned firsthand the pain of growing up amidst violence and alcohol abuse. Her escape from the problems of everyday life came through reading.

Later, as a police officer in Racine, Julia responded to many domestic violence calls and saw frightened children living with the pain she had known. And she noticed that in those children's homes there were rarely any books. Determined to share her own love of reading with those children, Julia founded a program called Cops 'N Kids Reading Center.

The program began with police officers giving kids books out of the trunks of their squad cars. Now it has grown into a thriving after-school program in Racine that has distributed more than 500,000 books to children. In 2000, Oprah Winfrey presented Julia with a Use Your Life Award, and in 2008, ABC News selected her as one of its Persons of the Year. The Cops 'N Kids organization now exists in more than seventy communities in the United States and overseas. In the essay that follows, Julia sends a special message to her young female readers.

Sister to Sister

Julia Burney-Witherspoon Speaks

I want to talk to you, my precious, dear little baby sister. Do you laugh when I call you my baby sister? But that's how I want you to think of yourself for a few minutes— my precious girl, with so much potential, so much living to do.

First of all, my sweet girl, if you do not have a baby yet, I beg you on my bended knees not to have one. Not for a long time. Not until you are financially and educationally prepared and have a husband by your side who wants to raise that baby with you.

But if you do have a baby, that changes everything. Whatever your age, you're not a little girl anymore. You're a mother. And I want to talk to you about being a *real mother*, not just a girl who has a baby. If you are going to do the right thing, you have to give up your life as a young girl. Things like going partying, chasing after boys, and hanging out with your friends are all in the past now. Does that sound harsh? Maybe you're saying, "But I'm just a teenager. I have a right to have some fun." But you stopped being just a teenager the day you decided to have that child. And your child deserves every bit of your time, your love, and your training.

Now, if you don't care about your child, that's different. If you aren't concerned about how he or she grows up, you just go on and live as you please. But if you're holding this book in your hands, I believe that you *do* care. And I believe that once you *know* better, you'll want to *do* better.

I know about being a young single mom. I was the oldest of twelve children. Our parents were hard-working and managed to keep us all fed, but they were so poor. There was a lot of drinking and a lot of fighting. Our parents loved us, but they did not express affection. By the time I was 17, when a boy came along saying, "I love you," I was hungry to believe it. Eventually, I was raising four children on my own.

Fortunately, every one of them turned out well. My son is in the military. My daughters are a police officer, a dentist, and a dental assistant. But their success didn't just happen. It happened because from the moment they were born I asked myself, What is it that I want for this child? What kind of adult do I want him or her to grow into? And I dedicated myself to working for those children, providing for them, and training them.

If you have a child, and you truly care for that child, you must dedicate yourself in that same way. Giving birth to a baby is not enough. Anybody can do that. But to be a real mother, a truly loving mother, you must start *today* to train that child. And training means many things. It means teaching manners—saying please and thank you. It means teaching the ABCs, how to tell time, how to tell colors. Training means establishing a bedtime routine, teaching respect for other people, making sure the child has memorized his or her phone number and address. Doing all those things, and doing them right, takes a huge amount of time, and you cannot do them and live like a young girl anymore. You can't. It's not possible.

(You notice that I'm talking about what *you* must do. I'm deliberately not talking about the baby's daddy or grandma or aunts. If you have dependable people in your life who are helping with the child, that's fine. But listen to me. Do *not* make the mistake of thinking it's okay to push the care of that child off on anyone else. Yes, the baby's father should help. But that's another topic. Right now I'm talking to you, the mother, and it's *your* responsibility to raise your child right.)

Let me tell you about some specific things that are important to do with your child. For starters, I want you to establish a regular bedtime routine with your child. Why is that important? Because how we go to sleep says so much about how we live. Some children go to sleep listening to Dad beating Mom. Some go to sleep hearing screams and fighting. Some go to sleep with people drinking and doing drugs in the next room. Is that what you want for your child? Or do you want your child to go to sleep feeling peaceful and loved, happy and cared for? If you do, make that happen. Decide, bedtime is at 7:30. I'll give my child a bath, and we'll snuggle in bed and read a story together. Make it a precious time, a happy ritual. It doesn't cost anything, and you'll be giving your child a lifetime of good memories.

Some other important things: Train your children to speak respectfully to adults. Teach them not to talk back—not to you, not to their grandparents, not to the lady in the store. If you tell them to pick up their toys and they yell, "No!" how do you think they'll act in school? Remember: In school they'll need to follow directions. They'll need to know how to sit quietly and listen. An undisciplined child cannot learn. It's up to you to bring discipline to your child's life. You can't expect anyone else to do it.

But discipline is not abuse. I am not telling you, "Beat the lessons into them." You must not do that. As a police officer, I know what a thin line there is between discipline and abuse. I've seen children scarred, burned with cigarettes, covered with welts from being whipped with extension cords, all in the name of discipline. True discipline is done with love. It's talking to your child. It's giving him a time out; it's taking away a toy or a privilege. Some people believe in paddling gently— maybe a tap on the hand with "No, no!" to get the child's attention. That's a personal choice. But do not beat your child. That is abuse, and if you do it, the state will take the child away from you. Beyond that, abused children often grow up to be abusers themselves. Or if they don't, they grow up to be deeply unhappy people with a kind of misery inside that their spouses and other loved ones may never understand.

I don't have a lot of space here, so I'm rushing through a few of the most important things a mother can do for her child. But next comes what I truly believe is the single most important thing of all.

Little Sister, I don't know if you are a reader. But whether you are or not, I beg you to make sure your children are. *Encouraging your children to read is the single most important thing you can do for them.* It will change their lives for the better in every possible way. It will determine how they do in school and on the job. It will allow them to read their paycheck, follow a recipe, pass a driver's test, read a map, apply for college, anything they need. Everything in modern society depends upon reading. If your child tells you, "I hate to read," you ignore that. Get your children library cards when they are babies, and use them. Turn off the TV, and sit down and read together!

Maybe you're saying, "But that isn't how I was raised at all. I don't know how to do this stuff." I wasn't raised that way either. I went to bed every night of my life stressed and scared. My parents were illiterate alcoholics. The police came to the house many a night to break up the fights. That doesn't matter. Cycles can only continue until one person says, "This stops here." I vowed to be that person. I decided from the moment my children were born that we would read together, that my children would never see me drunk or high, that they would never see a man hit me, that our home would be a place of peace. And you can do the same. No matter how you were raised, you have the choice how to raise your child. I'm going to say that again, loudly: *You have the choice how to raise your child.*

Breaking the cycle isn't easy. It won't make you popular with everyone. As my children were growing up, everyone in my world knew that the rules were different at my house. They knew that I would not let my children be exposed to drinking and fighting. My children would go to Grandma's with their little overnight bags, but if the drinking started, they had their orders to call me and I'd come get them. And I did so many a time and oh, did I catch holy hell for it. It made my siblings so angry. "There she goes, making her children out to be better than the rest of us," they'd say. To which I'd say, "Whatever. They're mine. I will protect them. I'm not raising them to please you."

Doing it right is hard work. But it's the most

important work you'll ever do. I'm fifty-eight years old, and I cannot tell you how much it means to me to see my children grown into successful, productive adults. It means everything to know they have good memories of their childhood. You have the power to do the same for your children. I hope and pray you will make use of that power.

Kimberly Roberts

About Kimberly Roberts

Kimberly Rivers Roberts and her husband, Scott Roberts, are residents of the Ninth Ward in New Orleans, Louisiana. For many people, the mention of New Orleans brings up images of Mardi Gras, Dixieland jazz, the French Quarter, and other tourist attractions.

But when Hurricane Katrina slammed into New Orleans in August 2005, the world saw another side of the city. While the middle-class and upper-class neighborhoods were quickly provided with emergency services, poor neighborhoods like the Ninth Ward were abandoned, their residents left to struggle for survival.

The amateur video shot by Kim during the days leading up to and during Hurricane Katrina became the centerpiece of an Oscar-nominated documentary film titled *Trouble the Water*. The documentary outraged viewers with its depiction of poor people being abandoned in a time of natural disaster. However, images of the courage, kindness, and determination of individual men and women gave the film an uplifting message.

Kim Roberts's own story and personality are at the heart of *Trouble the Water*. She shared the following account of her life, her experience with the film, and her family's hopes for the future in New Orleans.

Sister to Sister

Kimberly Roberts Speaks

I was born here in eastern New Orleans. My mom had three children—me and my two brothers. My mom and dad were together for a long time. Dad worked some as a carpenter, but he was basically a street hustler. Mom worked as a cook and a waitress. As far as I was concerned, when I was a little girl, things were pretty good. I was Daddy's girl, always with him. Mom was a good woman. She loved us, cooked for us, cleaned up, took care of Dad, helped us with school, hugged us and kissed us, and told us every day that she loved us. She did all that good mom stuff.

Then Daddy went off to prison and left her to fend for herself. She decided to move with me and my little brother to Florida, where her mother lived. I was 8. I had this fantasy of what Florida would be like—a new start, a new life. But my grandmother died three months after we got there. And Mom couldn't deal with how heavy her life had become. She turned to alcohol and drugs to get away from reality. Drugs stole her away from us. That's what drugs do. They take your self. It's like the drugs say, "You gimme that. Gimme your self. You won't be needing that no more."

Then she became sick. She couldn't take care of us the way she needed to, so that made me desperate to do so. Sometimes the lady that ran the local nail salon would let me clean the place up and give me $20. But I wasn't old enough to get a real job, so I'd steal. I had to fight, to carry a gun, to tote a knife. I talk about those days in my rap, "Amazing":

I'm singing "Mama don't cry
I know those rocks you're taking.
You been taking them every day
that's why the lights ain't on
Taking them every day since my daddy's gone
You been taking them every day,
won't leave them alone
You been taking them every day,
I'm in the danger zone. . . ."
Only thirteen years old I'm penitentiary prone . . .
I was just a little girl caught up in the storm
It still amazes me I lived to see myself grown.

It got so deep, so bad. By the time I was 13, the cops were looking for me for robbery, for passing bad checks, for purse snatching. We were living mostly on oranges with seasoned salt. We didn't have any lights; the electricity had been turned off. I knew I couldn't handle it anymore. I called the ambulance. We had a neighbor who managed to call my dad, who was out of prison by then. He made arrangements to fly me and my brother home to New Orleans once Mom was in the hospital.

When we got there, I imagined that things would be like they used to be between me and my dad, that I'd be his little girl again, but that didn't happen. I eventually found out that my mom had AIDS, and when she died, I wasn't allowed to mourn. So even though we were home again and had a parent there, things were pretty much the same as they had been with my mom. I was on my own. So I did what I knew how to do to survive: I hustled.

I was just 14 when I met Scott. He sent his boy over to speak to me, 'cause he was that shy. The guy said, "My boy likes you." After that, Scott started coming around. He was real respectful and sweet and walked on eggshells not to hurt me. I tell girls now, "You know how you know a guy is Mr. Right? Mr. Right is a giver; he gives to make you happy. He doesn't just take." Scott is my hero, my everything. We're married now, and we've got our baby girl, Skyy, who was born in January 2008.

So Scott and I were living in New Orleans, in the Ninth Ward, and in the summer of 2005 I bought a video camera from a guy for twenty bucks. I thought I'd have it to, you know, record family events, birthday parties, that kind of thing. Then we began to hear about this hurricane, Katrina, that was supposed to hit New Orleans. Everybody was talking about it. The mayor got on TV and said it was going to be real bad. He said, "Evacuate New Orleans." But what were people in places like the Ninth Ward supposed to do? We didn't have cars. There wasn't any plan to get the people out. We were on our own—kind of like I'd always been on my own. So I thought, Hey, if we're going to ride out this big-ass hurricane, I'll use the camera to tape what happens, and maybe we can make a few bucks selling it to a TV station or something afterwards.

So that's what I did. Scott and I and a bunch of our neighbors ended up trapped in our attic for two days while a whole lot of people around us died. I taped what I could. In case you don't know, Hurricane Katrina was one of the deadliest storms ever to hit the United States of America. Nearly every levee—levees are like dams that run along the banks of the Mississippi River to protect New Orleans—nearly every one of them broke down, flooding much of the city with water more than six feet deep. The levees had been neglected for years; the government knew they could collapse, but nothing was done about it. Nobody knows for sure how many people died in New Orleans, but it was more than 1,800. They were poor Black people, and they were left there to die. Two of them were my uncle and my grandmother. My uncle died in his house. My grandmother was in the hospital. The workers abandoned the hospital and let the old people die there. That's how it was.

A few days after the storm, Scott and I saw a film crew walking around. They had big cameras and stuff. Scott said, "They look important. Let's tell them about what we got." The people were Carl Deal and Tia Lessin, filmmakers from New York who wanted to make a film about Hurricane Katrina. We showed them our footage, and they ended up making *Trouble the Water*, a documentary about what Scott and I had experienced during the hurricane and afterwards. The film has done real well. It won the Grand Jury Prize at the Sundance Film Festival in Utah. (Skyy was born there in Utah, the day after the film's premiere.) It was nominated for an Academy Award for Documentary Feature. It's gotten great reviews. My raps are used in the soundtrack. I've put out a CD called *Troubled the Water* under my rap name, Black Kold Madina.

Since the film has come out, Scott's and my life have changed in some ways. We've been in more than fifteen different states helping to promote the movie. We've met a lot of people—Danny Glover, who was executive producer of the movie; Susan Sarandon, Isaiah Washington, Taye Diggs, Terry McMillan. At one of the parties we went to for the film, a woman came flying over and hugged me around the neck, saying, "Oh, the film was so great, I love your CD so much, you're so inspirational. . . ." I just said, "Well, thank you. I'm glad you liked them." Later Scott told me, "That was Rosario Dawson, that girl from the movie *Rent*."

So, you know, that's all been cool. And yeah, I hope some opportunities come our way because of the movie and the publicity that my music has gotten. But we don't want those opportunities to benefit only us.

This place—New Orleans, the Ninth Ward—is our home. We want to make things better for the people here. Maybe the movie will draw attention to how kids are living here, and other people will step forward to help. Maybe we can set up some kind of foundation to help the kids here.

Scott is mentoring young boys at the Y. We're doing what we can. We don't deal drugs anymore. Scott's working in construction. He's always been a hard worker; he just needed somebody to give him a chance. When we're driving around, he loves to point to buildings and say, "I helped build that."

Me, I'm performing my music and selling my CDs. And we're still getting invited to do speaking engagements and give interviews. I just came back from speaking at a college in Atlanta. That's pretty amazing. I dropped out of school in the tenth grade, and here I am talking to a group of college students.

Like I said in the movie, I stopped selling because I don't want to hold anybody down. What I mean is this: If I'm supplying you and you owe me money, my foot is on your neck, right? I may think that I'm rising, making money, but the fact is I can't go anywhere while I'm holding you down. You and I are trapped in the same cycle. And when you're a dealer in the hood, and people see you're doing well, they get jealous. In revenge, they'll take what's most precious to you. They'll touch your mother or your child or your little brother. They'll catch your old lady when she's alone. You gotta be an OG (Original Gangster) all the way. You have to be ready to kill. Eventually you will die or be killed or go to prison. That's no way to live. Scott and I, we told ourselves we were just in the business to make money, but that is never true. You can't pretend drug dealing is just another business. It's not. You're keeping people enslaved. You're keeping *yourself* enslaved.

The fact is, you can be addicted to money as much as to any drug. When you're poor, nobody teaches you to manage money. So you get some, and what do you do? You buy $1,000 shoes. You put diamonds on your fingers. You want white people to look at you and see that you've got it. But you know—he who shows his money has no money. That's living the poor person's lifestyle. You blow through your money, and what do you have to show for it? Some material objects that turn to rust and dust. Nothing that benefits you long term. In no time, you're back where you started from with nothing to show for yourself.

So what would I want to say to young ladies reading my words today? I'd say, Remember that nothing determines your future except you. Your world may be crashing down right now. As a child, you may not have much control over it. But when you get older and get the ball in your court, you can play a different game. Make a conscious decision that you are going to determine your own future. Make a decision to become the person that you want to be. If you stay positive, you can look ahead. I can say, "Yeah, I sold drugs. I did bad things in order to survive. That was then. This is now. I'm not going to be trapped by my past."

And take advantage of any chance you have to become educated. Without education, you have no control over your future. If you're ignorant, you'll spend your life dancing to someone else's music. And a big part of education is financial education. Learn how to handle money, how to budget, how to save.

Don't be held down by the things that happened to you that you couldn't control. Things may be rough now, but if you take control and stay positive, you can turn them around. Remember that a rose can grow out of a crack in the sidewalk. You can be that rose.

I'll leave you with some words from my rap, "Look Up":

I been through more than one Katrina in my life,
   and that's what's up
Then you say, Kold Madina, it ain't easy
And I say, things never stay the same
Come on and walk with me
Come on and talk with me
Come on and be with me
Until we all come up
So look up
And stay up
And look up
You heard me!

Mary Griffin

About Mary Griffin

For many years, Mary Griffin was a social worker in the city of Allentown, Pennsylvania. Her work brought her into constant contact with children and teenagers who she saw were hungry for love and the guidance of adults. She often felt frustrated that, as a city employee, she was limited in the role she could play in "her" children's lives.

Gradually, she found herself spending more and more hours outside of work acting as a substitute mother—going with children to parent-teacher conferences, attending school functions, or just sitting on the playground talking with children who needed a listening ear. Finally in 1996, she cashed in her life insurance policies to purchase a building in downtown Allentown and establish The Caring Place, an after-school center to provide children and teens with a safe, positive environment.

In the years since, The Caring Place has added a medical clinic, a clothing exchange, and support groups for people suffering from diabetes and sickle cell anemia. Mary and the other staffers help children with their homework, tutor them, and take them to museums and concerts and college campuses. The Caring Place provides services to more than 500 young people every year. Mary, her husband Steven, and their children live in Whitehall, Pennsylvania. Here, Mary talks to young ladies across the country about finding the strength to deal with troubles that may come their way.

Mary Griffin Speaks

This all began with my mother. She was a woman who took in anybody who needed help. There were always so many people at our dinner table that I stayed in a highchair until I couldn't fit into it anymore—eventually they just took the tray off and moved me up to the table. When we'd be out shopping, I'd hear people I didn't even know call my mother "Mom." She'd gone to school only through the sixth grade, but the knowledge she had was incredible.

My father died when I was 6, so Mother raised all five of us, plus my cousin and my oldest brother, who I call my "brother-uncle." His mother died when he was young, and my grandmother took him in. Then when *she* passed away, my mother raised him. And he's Caucasian, so when you look at our family pictures, it's a little surprising! So it is my mother's example that I was following when I opened The Caring Place, the youth development center that I run in Allentown,

Pennsylvania. My mother always believed you could care for one more. She'd say, "If there's food for five, there's food for ten. You just stretch it." She taught me so much about faith and about strength. Her attitude was always, "Okay, you're going through hard times right now. We don't know why such things have to happen. But it's up to you to turn it around."

I try to pass that attitude on to my girls at The Caring Place. I was so blessed to have women like my mother in my life from the beginning. Young girls need older women to help guide them through life, maybe to warn them about mistakes the women have made that they can help the girls avoid. Unfortunately, many young girls don't have relationships like that, so they pick up whatever information they can on the street, and often that information is not good.

The biggest area, I think, where girls pick up bad information is about having babies at a young age. I hear all the reasons they give. They tell me, for instance, "I don't want to be an old mom. I want to have my babies while I'm still young enough to have fun with them." They don't think, I need to get *myself* together first, and prepare myself to care for a child. There's no thought of *how* am I going to provide for this child? How will I give it a decent place to live?

Or they'll tell me, "I need somebody who loves me." Maybe that's a reason to get a puppy, but it's not a good reason to have a baby!

They tell me they need to have a baby in order to keep a guy around. I'll say, "But, sweetie, you know that guy already has two babies with two other girls. It didn't work for them, did it?" And they'll say, "But this is different. He loves me."

Sometimes their moms are actually encouraging the girls because they want to be young grandmas. They can't have babies anymore, so their daughters have them and the moms raise them. Then the girl is back out there with another boy, and there's another baby, and it goes on. We have one young lady who's been in and out of The Caring Place for years. She's 22 and pregnant with her sixth child. I saw her and said, "Oh, honey, not again. You know the last guy didn't treat you right." She said, "But it's okay this time, Miss Mary; this guy is working." But she was coming here every day for food. In her case, the children were eventually taken away. What kind of future will those children have?

When we talk about having babies, I try to give my girls another perspective. I encourage them to get their education, to prepare themselves for life before they become mothers. Or if they aren't into education, to at least get a job and be able to buy the things they need before they have a child. I say, "Make sure you can take care of *yourself* and that you really know who you're having this baby with. Be sure this is a good man who will stay with you." I want to say "a good husband," but I know this isn't the way many of the girls have been taught to think. Times have changed. Not long ago, if a young lady got pregnant, she was *gone*. She left the community she lived in because being single and pregnant was so shameful. I wouldn't want it to be that way again, but on the other hand, it shouldn't be such an everyday thing for young girls to have babies.

The sad thing is that having babies so young, as if it's no big deal, reflects the way these young ladies view themselves—as if *they* don't matter. They don't respect themselves, so they don't take care of themselves. I know that learning to love and respect yourself is hard if you've grown up in a family that's treated you poorly, as many girls have. It's hard if you've had many harsh words thrown at you. If no one has shown you respect, you may not know what respect is. That's why when a girl comes to The Caring Place, we try to take baby steps in that direction, by doing things as simple as saying "You look so pretty today." When you treat a young lady with respect, you slowly begin to see self-respect blossom within her.

Sister to Sister

How can you tell when a woman has self-respect? She will not treat herself as if she were trash. She understands that her body is a gem, a treasure that she honors and cares for. She realizes that it is not something cheap and meaningless that should be given to just anyone. If you're going to give someone a gift, it should be something special, like the engagement ring that a man gives his fiancée. Once you start treating yourself like something common, your self-esteem suffers and everything goes downhill. But if a young lady learns to respect *herself,* everything else falls into place.

One of the best things a young woman can do for herself on the journey to self-respect is to find older women in her life to model herself after. If there aren't women like that close at hand, she has to do a little looking. I tell my girls, "Look to your teachers. Look to the women in your church. If you're at the hairdresser and women are sitting around talking, look for women who seem to have their lives somewhat together. They don't have to be perfect, but if they have qualities you admire, find ways to spend time with them. Associate yourself with people you want to be like. Find women who understand that there are certain things you need to do in order to get what you want in life—such things as working to get a home, as opposed to settling for being on public assistance and living in the projects.

Surround yourself with such people. Learn from their examples."

As you learn and grow, you may find yourself running into some resistance from the people closest to you. What happens in your own home may not be the best. I know. I've seen it all. I've had girls here, thirteen or fourteen years old, who were prostituting themselves—and that was okay with their mom as long as they brought the money home. What I'd encourage you to do is tell yourself, "What happens at home doesn't define me." And it's a wonderful thing to look at the other women in your family, maybe women who have not found the strength to do what you're doing, and think, I'm able to step out of here, but I'll come back for you. Unless you're in a situation where you're in danger and really have to get out, don't totally separate yourself from your family. Try your best to achieve what you need in order to become a good woman, but then go back to help your mother or grandmother. Take the good things you've achieved—your education, your job—and use those things to show them a better way. Go back and teach them the things you've learned.

I've been doing the work I do long enough that I know the devastation that can happen in a young woman's life if she doesn't take care of herself. The things I see girls go through—I don't know how I would handle it at their age, mentally or emotionally. They are stronger than they think they are, because they *are* enduring those things. That's what I would like to tell any young ladies who are in difficult situations: "You are stronger than you know. Take that strength that allows you to survive the bad things. Find it. Feel it. Make it work for you. Draw on it to create a better future for yourself."

Hamidah Sharif-Harris

About Hamidah Sharif-Harris

Hamidah Sharif-Harris holds a bachelor's degree from Adelphi University as well as two master's degrees and a doctorate from Columbia University in New York. Her accomplishments would be impressive for anyone, but they are particularly surprising when you learn that she barely managed to graduate from high school. As the daughter of a strict but supportive Muslim mother, and sister of two academic "superstars," Hamidah was the family rebel—until she realized the game she was playing would hurt only herself. Today Dr. Sharif-Harris is Assistant Professor of Health Education at Coppin State University in Baltimore. She and her husband, Ishmael, are the parents of a daughter, Naelah. They live in Owings Mills, Maryland.

Hamidah Sharif-Harris Speaks

When I was a little girl growing up in Harlem, we were part of a supportive, good-sized Muslim community. We children had lots of "aunts" and "uncles" and "cousins" around. My mother was respected. Our house was the one where friends and neighbors would naturally congregate. My older sisters, Khadijah and Asia, were always strong, faithful Muslim women.

But somewhere along the way, things changed. People started disappearing, leaving the area. The local Muslim church stopped offering many programs. Our Muslim elementary school closed. And my father was in and out of our lives. Maybe those are some reasons that I lost my way.

I felt out of place, out of step with my peers. I had plenty of issues. To begin with, there was my name. I hated it! Nobody pronounced it right. When my name was called at a school assembly, they'd always mess it up. It's pronounced *ham MEE dah sha REEF*. But they'd say, "Will *HAM i duh SHER riff* come forward?" and I'd want to crawl under my seat. One time after an elementary school play, we kids were supposed to introduce ourselves. My mother sat there proudly waiting for me to speak. I stepped forward and said loud and clear, "My name is Tamika Jones."

And holidays! In the 1980s, the in-school celebration of Christmas was huge. But my mom was determined that I was not going to be involved. I couldn't even cut a Christmas tree out of green construction paper. I was an outcast! Luckily, I had one little friend who was a Jehovah's Witness and was not allowed to participate either, so we'd sit there together and make sad puppy faces. (Later on, my mom lightened up on the holiday rules. I was allowed to dress up for Halloween, for instance, as long as I was something nice like a fairy or a princess or a ballerina.)

We didn't wear traditional Muslim clothing like head coverings, but we were required to dress modestly. I couldn't wear miniskirts, and oh, how I wanted one! In fact, if we wore skirts at all, we had to wear pants underneath—*not* stylish. Mostly, we wore long dresses. And we didn't eat pork, which kids enjoyed teasing me about in the cafeteria.

And, of course, my older sisters were perfect. I don't mean that in a sarcastic way. They really were. They are my role models to this day. Asia is an educator and an author with her own consulting company. Khadijah is a vice president and general counsel for BET, Black Entertainment Television.

To top it off, I had big complexion issues. My mom is light-skinned; I'm three or four shades darker than she is. I got used to hearing people say, "Oh. *She's* your daughter?"

Anyway, for whatever reasons, as I got into my teens, I began to rebel. If my family was respected for being upright and hard-working, I was going the other way. I started hanging out with people I had no business hanging out with. I spent a lot of time with one girl in particular who I thought had it made. At age 13 she'd say, "I'm going out," and her mother would just say, "Okay." My mother, on the other hand, gave me the third degree. "Where are you going? How are you getting there? What's a phone number where I can reach you? Who else will be there?" Later, I found out that my friend's mother was a crack addict, but at the time, I thought she was the coolest mom.

I started hanging out on the streets of Harlem until all hours, to the point that my mother called the police a number of times to look for me. Khadijah had been the absolute top scholar at my high school. I didn't feel capable of competing with that, so I decided to excel in the other direction—I would *fail* every class. I cut school constantly. Finally Mom began driving me to school herself and seeing me through the front door. But I'd just wait a few minutes and duck out the back. I spent my days roaming around Central Park, Orchard Beach, wherever. But usually I went to see my boyfriend, James.

Of course, as a sixteen-year-old Muslim girl, I was not supposed to have a serious relationship with a boy. My mother reminded me again and again that my only thoughts should be about school and going to college, as my older sisters were doing. I liked the idea of going to college, but I wasn't doing anything to make that idea a reality. Instead I filled my head with dreams of James. His attention filled the hole in my heart where my father's love should have been. He was my everything. Soon after we began dating, he told me he loved me. "If you really love me, you'll show it," he said.

Show it? I thought. How? He told me. "But I'm a Muslim," I told him. "We don't do that before marriage."

"Maybe you don't really love me," he answered.

He kept bringing the subject up. He told me it was okay because we loved each other. It was okay because we probably would get married someday. Since we were going to be together, it didn't matter if we waited or not.

This decision was a huge one for me. I thought and thought about it. I was terrified of what my mother would say if she found out. On the other hand, I was terrified that James would leave me if I said no. I made myself believe that he loved me and I loved him, so everything would be all right. Finally I went to the health center for birth control. I told James yes.

Not long after we started our relationship, I cut school and went to his house, and we spent the entire day together. As we left his house, a girl came up the sidewalk. James looked surprised to see her—surprised and guilty. "Hi!" he said to her, sounding nervous. Gesturing to me, he said, "This is my classmate, Hamidah."

I stared at him in disbelief. "Your *classmate*?" I said, "I'm not your classmate! I'm your girlfriend!" Seeing James's face, I knew the truth. I began to cry. Through my sobs I heard James tell the other girl he had no idea why I was so upset. He swore on his mother's grave that I was nothing but a friend from school. He and the girl walked away together.

It was the most devastating moment of my life. I cried because I had given James something precious, something that he had treated cheaply. I cried because I had betrayed myself and my values. I cried remembering all the times my mother had told me that I was born with a purpose in this world. She had said, "Remember those who lived before you and sacrificed everything so that you could achieve your dreams." I cried thinking about my name: *Hamidah* means "one who gives praise to Allah," and *Sharif* means "honorable and respected." I didn't hate my name anymore. Instead, I felt that I didn't deserve it.

Not long after that day, at the end of my junior year, report cards came out. I was hanging with my homegirls, my bad girls, and we compared our awful grades. "Whatever," one said. Another carelessly said, "I'm going to drop out and get my GED later."

Then I heard my other friends, the ones who had brains and used them, talking about taking the SATs and applying for college. And it was like I suddenly woke up out of a dream. I thought, What? SATs? It's time to do that? Reality slapped me in the face. I realized, If I'm going to go to college, I need to get to work!

It was a clear-cut fork in the road. I could no longer hang out with my bad girls, and boys could not be part of my life at this point. I cut them all out.

The next year was the hardest of my life. I took a full load of classes during the day and another full load at night. During the summer I did the same. I literally finished all four years of high school in one year—yes, I had failed *that* many classes. I made a lot of sacrifices that year. My friends would go off to parties and hear from me, "No, I have a biology test tomorrow." They couldn't believe it. But I could not bear the thought of staying on the same road I'd been traveling, and spending the rest of my life in Harlem. This wasn't today's Harlem, Bill Clinton's Harlem. This was dirty old, trash-blowing-in-your-face, crack-everywhere Harlem. It was a hard, hard place to live, and I wanted to get out.

Later, in college and then graduate school, as I read about heroes like Harriet Tubman and Frederick Douglass and how they struggled to advance our people, I understood what my mother was trying to give me. I understood why she had pushed me so hard. I thought she was just deeply uncool and trying to mess up my adolescence. But somehow, despite raising five kids on public assistance in Harlem, she had been able to look over the horizon and see something positive to strive for. Today she has my college diplomas hanging on *her* wall. She says, "You got the education. These are mine." She deserves them.

Lina Buffington

Lina Buffington

About Lina Buffington

A native of Detroit, Michigan, Lina grew up as the eldest girl in her family and as caretaker for her younger cousins. At the age of 18, she moved to Atlanta, Georgia, to attend Spelman College. She made Atlanta her home for ten years, earning her master's and doctor's degrees in philosophy from Emory University.

In Atlanta, Lina also became involved with Nzinga and Ndugu, a rites-of-passage organization focused on instilling principle and character in African American young people. It was through her involvement in Nzinga and Ndugu that she met Michael Alexander, the man who would become her husband. Lina's growing interest in being an advocate for youth steered her away from her original plan of teaching philosophy.

In July 2006, she accepted the post as Director of College Retention and Success with Philadelphia Futures, a nonprofit organization that prepares students to move to and through college. In that position, she advises over 200 Philadelphia Futures students attending colleges and universities throughout the country. Lina and her husband live in the East Oak Lane area of Philadelphia.

Sister to Sister

As Lina's essay shows, even an academic high achiever, a young woman who outwardly seems to have it all together, can be racked by serious self-doubt.

Lina Buffington Speaks

Dear Little Sister,

Hello, my dear. There are so many things that I would like to share with you. First, I want to tell you how beautiful you are. Watching you grow up has been one of the greatest blessings in my life. When you were little, I loved to see you running around with those little puffball ponytails. You were so comfortable in your own skin, so vibrant and unselfconscious. It did not seem like you were afraid of anything.

One of my biggest fears has been that someday you would learn from the music videos and fashion magazines that little Black girls are not, and have never been, the ideal. Now that you have learned about "good hair" and "bad hair," and about the relationship between skin color and beauty in the Black community, I feel like I have to be especially vigilant in my affirmation of your beauty. Though it may not mean a lot coming from me at this time in your life, I feel the need to say it anyway. You have always been—and will always be—precious and beautiful to me. In fact, you are the one who helped me begin to look at *myself* differently. When I look into your face and see a little bit of me in you, maybe in the way you smile, I feel a little more beautiful.

I know that it may seem like I don't understand you because we don't share the same tastes in music or clothes, but I do understand you. One of the reasons I complain about the music that you listen to and the videos that you watch is that I am afraid. I remember how those things affected me when I was your age. I remember how fat, inadequate, and ugly I felt seeing the girls on the videos. I haven't told you that before. I've wanted so much to set a good example for you, and in my mind that meant being independent, successful, and strong. So how could I tell you about my fears and insecurities? But the fact is, by the time I was your age I already knew beyond a shadow of a doubt that I was ugly.

"She so ugly."

I was at Eastland Mall right outside of Detroit with my younger cousin. We were in one of the department stores when two older girls walked by. One of them turned to look at me and said to the other with a cold giggle, "She so ugly." I remember I was wearing long thick "Dukie" braids, like the ones that Janet Jackson wore in the movie *Poetic Justice*. I had done them myself because I could not afford to go to the beauty shop. I had gotten really good at doing them. The braids were one of the things that I did to try to be at least a little stylish or trendy, so the remark was especially painful. Also, my younger cousin was with me, and she heard the comment. No one would ever call her ugly with her light-brown "yellow" complexion and slanted eyes.

I can't remember exactly how I responded. I did not say anything back, and I could not cry there in the store in front of the older girls and my cousin, but I know I wanted to. I probably cried later that night. I often cried myself to sleep and woke up puffy-eyed in the morning. This was a habit that continued well into adulthood—crying in private, in silence. I swallowed down whatever it was that I felt, swallowed it down and stuffed it deep into the pit of my gut. Doing this for years led to chronic stomach problems and heartburn.

"Her? She's ugly."

One of the popular girls in class sat three rows ahead of me and threw a dismissive glance over her shoulder. There was no scorn in her voice; she simply stated a fact.

Early on, I decided that, because I would never be beautiful—not even cute—I would have to be the smartest, best, and brightest at everything else. I shone academically, and I won awards for my writing and first-place medals in clarinet solo competitions. I was a student leader at school and a responsible, efficient daughter and eldest cousin. I worked, babysat my cousins, and was always at the top of my class. I got a scholarship to college and supported myself throughout. I tried very, very hard to be good enough, to fill in the gaps left by the ugliness that I felt was at the root of my loneliness.

Ugly girls do not go to prom or get invited to parties. Ugly girls go to the movies with friends or alone. They do not have teenage love affairs or spend hours primping in front of the mirror. For an ugly girl, the mirror is the greatest enemy. A great deal of time is spent avoiding the mirror, even a reflection in store windows and glass doors. Some days, though, I lingered before the mirror, trying to identify the root of my ugliness. Was it my broad nose? The eyes that were not hazel, green, or slanted? Was it the cheeks that sat round and low on my face, dimple-free, rather than being perched high atop prominent cheekbones? Was it my unremarkable lips, not plump enough to be considered seductive? Was it my skin, too brown for me to be mistaken for anything but a descendant of Africans?

"All of the above!" shouted back the magazine models, music-video girls, and movie stars. My ugliness was confirmed by the absence of anyone that looked like me on television or in the movies (unless she was the mama, the maid, or the butt of a joke). My ugliness was reflected in popular culture and in the eyes of my peers.

In my family I was the tallest, the darkest, the fattest . . . the *ugliest*, so I saw it there, too.

I will tell you a secret, Little Sister, one that it has taken me many, many years to learn: The mirror cannot tell you anything about beauty; it is a dead thing. It is flat and one-dimensional, and can capture only one perspective at a time. It can only mimic your multidimensional reality. Magazine and video images are edited, airbrushed, retouched. Like mirrors, they are dead and one-dimensional. They reflect the perspective of the photographer, producer, makeup artists, and more. They tell you only a small part of a complicated story. They will never take you beyond the outermost surface of the women that they represent. They capture only partial truths about a person, so they will teach you nothing about beauty.

There is a cliché that says "Beauty is only skin deep." That is not true. Cuteness may be skin deep, but beauty is soul deep. That is why flat images can never tell you anything about how beautiful you are. Think about it—what makes green eyes or blue eyes any more "beautiful" than brown eyes? What makes yellow hair more "beautiful" than black hair? Really think about it. Who are the people in your life that you think are beautiful—not just cute or sexy or pretty—but really beautiful? What is it about those people that makes them beautiful to you? Is it just their skin color or the shape of their nose?

The all-female singing group, Sweet Honey in the Rock, sings a song called "No Mirrors in My Nana's House":

There were no mirrors in my Nana's house,
no mirrors in my Nana's house.
There were no mirrors in my Nana's house,
no mirrors in my Nana's house.
And the beauty that I saw in everything
was in her eyes (like the rising of the sun).
I never knew that my skin was too black.
I never knew that my nose was too flat.
I never knew that my clothes didn't fit.
I never knew there were things that I'd missed,
cause the beauty in everything
was in her eyes (like the rising of the sun);
. . . was in her eyes.

I often think about this song and wonder what it would be like to live in a world with no mirrors. How would you feel if what you knew about yourself came from the people who love you? How would you see yourself if there were no mirrors to look into? What would it be like if your mother and her mother before her had never learned to dislike their skin color or hair texture? What if fashion models looked like the women that you see in the grocery store or on your block?

Neither you nor I can wave a magic wand and transform the world into one like I imagine. But we can do something almost as good. Who are the people in your life that are loving and supportive? Who are the people who are willing to tell you the truth about yourself and hold you accountable to a high standard? Surround yourself with those people. Let them be your mirrors.

I have found my own mirrors. When I look into the eyes of my husband, I can see the beauty in myself reflected in his love for me. When I look into your eyes, Little Sister, I can see the beauty in myself reflected in your beauty. When I look into the eyes of my friends, I can see the beauty in myself reflected in their respect for me. Look into my eyes, Little Sister, and you will know that you are beautiful and wonderful and perfect. You are perfect in your fear and in your anger. You are perfect in your uncertainty and in your frustration. You are perfect in your brilliance and in your courage.

I will tell you something else, Little Sister. I debated whether I would write about this because it is not something that a lot of people know about me. I decided that I would tell you because I never want you to be ashamed of anything about yourself. I suffer from anxiety and depression. For so long I have been ashamed of this—so much so that I failed to get the help that I needed for a very long time. I used to think that people who said that they were depressed were just weak. When I was diagnosed, I thought that I could overcome depression by willing it away. I thought that if I just ate right and exercised and took vitamins and prayed, I would no longer be depressed. Like so many Black people who suffer from mental illnesses, I have been silent about it. I am afraid that others will be as harsh as I once was and will think that I am weak.

I believe that all of those years of internalizing self-hatred and biting back my emotions contributed to my depression. All those years of hiding in the bathroom to cry and putting on a mask of confidence and self-assurance meant that I was not telling the truth, not even to myself. I never learned how to be honest about my emotions or how to deal with them in a healthy way. I was ashamed of my fears and my sadness. That shame made me even more afraid and sad, leading to a cycle that required more lies and more hiding.

I went to see my first therapist as a freshman at Spelman College but did not see anyone regularly until graduate school, which is when I was officially diagnosed and received a prescription for medication. I did not actually begin taking medication until 2007, when I had hit rock bottom and the illness began to affect my body. I took an antidepressant for a year, but because of the side effects, I recently decided to stop and reevaluate my options. Right now I am trying to decide what my next steps will be. Each day that I make the decision to eat well, to rest, to take care of myself, and to treat myself with loving-kindness is a victory. Slowly, I am coming to recognize in myself the beautiful woman that I see when I look in your eyes.

This transformation will not happen overnight. To this day, I am still learning that it has never been the good grades or awards, not my education or my career that makes me worthy of love and care. I am worthy simply because I am a child of the Creator. I am worthy because I was blessed with a life and put on this earth with a purpose. While there is no single formula for learning how to love oneself, I would like to offer a short list of tools that I have acquired over the years. I hope something in this list will resonate with you and help you on your journey:

1. **Don't suffer in silence.** Silence kills. I know that being vulnerable can be scary and uncomfortable. That is something I still struggle with, but I have seen how suffering in silence damages my mind, body, and spirit.

Silence does not make me stronger. It does not protect me from future harm. All silence does is prevent me from getting the help and support that I need. One technique that I use in order to communicate things that are painful to talk about is to write letters. Sometimes when I cannot find the words to speak, I explain my feelings in a letter to a friend. I have also found that when I am afraid to talk to friends or family, it can be very helpful to talk to a therapist, spiritual advisor, or mentor. If you have no one else to turn to, you can always write to me:

Lina Buffington
Philadelphia Futures
230 S Broad, 7th floor
Philadelphia, PA 19126

2. **Get creative.** Find a passion, something that you love to do even if you are not "good" at it, because being "good" is not the point. You might love to sing, dance, sew, write, act, draw, paint, or take pictures. All that matters is that it is something that makes you feel fulfilled. Being creative is a way for you to find your voice and express your feelings. One of the things that I love to do now is sew. In college I taught myself

how and began to make clothing and quilts. I also love to sculpt, make pottery, and garden. When I am doing any of these things, I feel at peace. It feels wonderful to create things—to turn bits of cloth into a quilt, to shape a lump of clay into a bowl, or to sow seeds in dirt and watch them grow into flowers.

3. **Find a sister circle.** It breaks my heart when I hear young women say that they do not have women friends or that they do not get along with other women. Having close "sister-friends" has always been my saving grace. During all of the lowest points of my life, I have been able to depend on my sisters. I know that they love me for who I am and not for how I look or for what they think they might be able to get from me. I learn a lot about myself through my friendships with these women. If you have a hard time developing friendships with other young women, consider joining an organization like Girls Inc. or a local Rites of Passage organization for young women.

4. **Talk kindly to yourself.** How do you speak to the people who you love and respect a great

deal? I often have to ask myself that question. I would never call my mother stupid. I would never look my husband in the face and tell him that he is ugly and fat. I would never call you a dumb-ass if you made a mistake. So why do I talk to *myself* that way? This is probably one of the hardest habits to break because it is so automatic. Here's a very powerful exercise I once read about: Imagine yourself as a child. Comfort that child and talk to her. I tried it, and I talked very lovingly to myself. It was very strange, and it made me cry. I had never spoken to myself in such a kind way. This exercise really made me understand how much I hurt myself with the daily insults that I subject myself to. Speak kindly to yourself! You deserve loving-kindness.

5. **Be healthy.** In order to be your best self, you have to take care of your body. Drink lots of water, eat fruits and vegetables, get plenty of sleep, and be active. When you fill your body with junk (soft drinks, processed foods, fast food, candy) you *feel* like junk. Find a physical activity that you enjoy. It could be walking, playing an organized sport, running, dancing,

or weightlifting. The activity does not matter; what matters is that you stay active. I am most consistent when I go to the gym, so I work out three or four times a week. When I am regularly active, I can feel the difference not only physically but also in terms of my attitude and energy.

6. **Say no to toxic relationships.** If you are in a relationship that leaves you feeling drained, anxious, afraid, or unhappy, this is a toxic relationship. The relationship could be with a boyfriend or girlfriend, a friend, or even a relative. I understand that this can be very difficult, especially when the relationship involves a family member. If there is abuse or violence in a relationship, it should be cut off completely. If you are in a situation that you feel is dangerous and you are not sure how to get out of it, contact the National Domestic Violence Hotline for guidance (1-800-799-7233 or TTY 1-800-787-3224). If the relationship is not one in which you feel threatened, you might simply need to set more boundaries, like limiting the amount of time that you spend talking to that person. Your relationships should feed you in some positive way. If you surround yourself with positive and loving people, it will be so much easier for you to learn how to be kind and loving to yourself.

7. **Most important, be patient and gentle with yourself.** Growth does not happen overnight. Give yourself the space to make mistakes.

As you can see, learning how to love myself has been a process. You, my dear little sister, are one of the reasons that I finally decided to seek help and begin this journey. You have so much faith in me, and my love for you is greater than my fear. I know that if I am to help you overcome all of the negativity that is in the world, I have to do a better job of taking care of myself. I cannot just tell you to love yourself. I have to show you what loving oneself looks like, even when it is hard. That is why I decided to write you this letter, Little Sister. I want you to know that it is okay to struggle and that your problems do not make you any less wonderful. Sometimes it is our struggles that force us to discover the depths of our beauty.

Someday you will have a little sister, a younger cousin, a little girl in your classroom or neighborhood, or even your own little daughter. One day she will come to you and look into your eyes so that she can see herself. What will she see?

> *There were no mirrors in my Nana's house,*
> *no mirrors in my Nana's house.*
> *There were no mirrors in my Nana's house,*
> *no mirrors in my Nana's house.*
> *And the beauty that I saw in everything*
> *was in her eyes (like the rising of the sun).*
> *Chil', look deep into my eyes.*
> *Chil', look deep into my eyes.*